OBLIQUE
VERDICTS

OBLIQUE
VERDICTS

JAMES CLARKE

Publishers of Singular
Fiction, Poetry, Nonfiction, Drama, Translations and Graphic Books

Library and Archives Canada Cataloguing in Publication

Clarke, James, 1933-, author
Oblique verdicts / James Clarke.

Poems.
Issued in print and electronic formats.
ISBN 978-1-55096-662-6 (softcover).--ISBN 978-1-55096-663-3 (EPUB).--
ISBN 978-1-55096-664-0 (Kindle).--ISBN 978-1-55096-665-7 (PDF)

I. Title.

PS8555.L37486O24 2017   C811'.54   C2016-907515-X
                                             C2016-907516-8

Published by Exile Editions Ltd ~ www.ExileEditions.com
144483 Southgate Road 14 – GD, Holstein, Ontario, N0G 2A0.
Printed and Bound in Canada by Marquis.

We gratefully acknowledge the Canada Council for the Arts, the Government
of Canada, the Ontario Media Development Corporation, and the
Ontario Arts Council for their support toward our publishing activities.

Canadian Sales: The Canadian Manda Group, 664 Annette Street,
Toronto ON M6S 2C8   www.mandagroup.com   416 516 0911

North American and International Distribution, and U.S. Sales:
Independent Publishers Group, 814 North Franklin Street,
Chicago IL 60610 www.ipgbook.com toll free: 1 800 888 4741

My gratitude to James R. Elkins for his honest, devoted, and inspired work on this collection.

I dedicate this collection to Susan Musgrave, Barry Callaghan and James R. Elkins.

A WORLD APART

PARODIES OF HOLY WRIT

SMALL MERCIES

WHISPER OF DOUBT

AN ICY NUMBING WIND

THE JUDGE GROWS OLD

GOING HOME

FOREWORD

by JAMES R. ELKINS

I read no more poetry than I did mailing advertisements, until I got hooked, that is until I found poetry that felt as necessary to me as the short stories and novels that have always been a part of my reading, and in recent years, central to my work as a teacher. I regret that I allowed so many good reading years elapse in ignorance of the kind of evocative poetry that James Clarke writes. I find it, now, quite unimaginable that I let poetry—this great gift—sit outside on my doorstep so long.

I am fortunate to have stumbled upon James Clarke's poetry. For me, and I suspect for most readers, the bulk of the poetry that comes our way lacks appeal: the poems don't work and they don't work for myriad reasons. Simply put, most poetry is easily ignored and all too readily forgotten. Poetry is a great deal like music; we dislike far more of it than we find appealing. The challenging task with poetry, even more so than with music, is to find poems that mean something to us, poems that work for us and work on us—poems that we want to read and return to again and again. The imperative for me in reading poetry is clear: *I want to find poetry that means something to me.* Jim Clarke's poems meet this criteria. What we find in Clarke's poetry is a man who looks honestly and with great clarity at his life's work and the legal and emotional world he inhabits.

This is poetry that reflects not only the poet's search for meaning but our own.

My interest in poetry was sparked when I discovered the work of John William Corrington, a novelist and English professor, who decided at age 40 to become a lawyer. One of the things that most intrigued me about Corrington—let's say it caught my eye—he was a well-published poet before he became a lawyer. Reading Corrington, I assumed (knowing far more about lawyers than I did about poets) that lawyers and poets existed in different realms of thought and feeling, and that following the path of the poet would make such a person a stranger in the lawyer's world. In this era of John Grisham and Scott Turow, we may have grown accustomed to the idea of the lawyer as novelist, but there is still some mystery, and perhaps a sense of puzzlement at the idea of someone who can manage to be both a lawyer and a poet. No one has managed to bridge the great divide in these two seemingly different worlds better than James Clarke.

As both poetry and law are acquired tastes, it is all the more surprising to find these quite distinctive tastes in a single person, with a single mind, and a single life to live. I was so taken by what at one time I found to be the oddness of the idea of the *lawyer poet* that when I discovered these two worlds of being in the work of John William Cor-rington, I spent a decade identifying America's lawyer poets—living and dead—and set about to publish in the *Legal Studies Forum*, a journal that I edit, the best poetry of our contemporary lawyers. What I've learned in a decade and a half of publishing the work of lawyer poets is that most of them do not make their lives as lawyers a part of their poetry. And yes, a special few, like Judge Clarke, find a way to avoid the wall of separation between their lives as poets and their lives as lawyers. In 2012, Judge Clarke gave me the honor of allowing me to publish a collection of his poems in the *Legal Studies Forum*, and we followed that first collection, with five additional collections. To my knowledge, these were the first and only collections of judge-inspired poetry published in the United States. In 2013, I edited an anthology, *Lawyer Poets and That World We Call Law: An Anthology of Poems about the Practice of Law*, in which James Clarke's poetry was prominently featured.

❦

When we educate lawyers, the focus is on the work of judges. Law teachers present judicial opinions to students with the idea that these opinions are the source of legal rules and legal doctrines from which the student will learn *the law*. The focus for the student is the *law* found in the judicial opinion, not the *persons* and *human relationships* deeply embedded and disguised in the legal language of the judicial opinion. Still further disguised is the simple fact that the judge who writes the opinion is a *person*. The student's image—and expectations—of a judge are shaped by a volatile mix of stereotypes, TV images, and a modicum of reality that they distill from reading a judge's legal opinions. In the mind of the student, the judge—black-robed, steeped in the intricacies of the law, powerful, objective, umpire of legal disputes—is an oracle of the law. What law schools fail to teach is that the judge is a *person* who has a life and a mind that can never be fully and entirely defined by the *law*. In language that is strikingly distinct from the legal language in which lawyers and judges traffic, James Clarke has written an unprecedented collection of poems about the human side of judging.

For decades, I have been asking my students: *What does it mean to be a lawyer?* Now, in the poems collected here— an extraordinary and evocative collection of memorable and soulful poetry—Judge Clarke answers a variation of that question—*what does it mean to be a judge?* For anyone familiar with lawyer stereotypes, anyone who might want a glimpse of the arcane world of lawyers and legal practices, Judge Clarke's reflective excavations of the person behind the lawyer persona provide insight into one man's struggle to wed legal thinking with the compassion that we hope to find in our judges.

STORM FRONT

Augury

Beckoned by the mysterious world of grownups
we yearned for the end of school days when we

could begin our journey on the bright road of
dreams, bridled at the tyranny of nuns who'd

make us stay after school to clean blackboards &
brushes in punishment for our small transgressions

till freed at last we'd trudge home, hands coated &
clothing faded, faces chalky white, our first, faint

augury of the blizzard of whiteness that awaited us
on the hidden road ahead.

Sisyphus's Stone

Day after day,
between morning's spilt coffee &
evening's ragged return

we gather in the vestibule
of the heart
for another lesson
in the hard art
of loving,

which no one
fully masters, but
keeps trying, hoping
to be someday what we aspire
to be next,

tomorrow after tomorrow.

Commemoration

I spin memories
out of thinnest air,
nail them
to the walls of my house
with the invisible
hammer of love,
listen to the music
of times lost
as they fade & leak away,
knowing how everything
is mediated & contingent,
the hammer lives only in me &
one day, alas,
house, hammer & I
will part company:
the day the music dies.

What Slips Away

After the initial shock
    the water is perfect;
sun, the young virtuoso
    of the day, dances
under the wind's
    bright wings; our
children, now grown,
    brows notched
with care, watch, as
    we once watched,
their own children,
    frolic & splash in
the waves.

But the shining
    gaiety doesn't last;
our lives are a constant
    arriving & emptying
out, the unique
    moments that touch us
most deeply
    linger & then slip away
to return at odd moments
    or not at all.
Much is lost
    in the tangled net of memory.

Missing Keys

In the seniors' residence
the widows, pale faces
    strafed with age,
sense the universe shutting down,
eat in silence in the dining room,
fidget with their forks, stare around
the room with forlorn blankness.

Then, like the moon on a winter's
night edging through rifts of clouds,
they cautiously push their walkers down
long, unending corridors, tired eyes
full of questions, wondering
    where they put the keys
to their lost homes.

At the Funeral Home

I arrive early, wait in the vestibule. "Funerals Let Us Say Goodbye" reads the message in the pale-gold frame above the reception desk. The Director ushers me into a room with washed-out light, the smell of furniture polish.

You're laid out on a gurney in your good blue pinstriped suit, your mouth clamped shut, all your well-mapped lines of living expunged from brow & cheeks. I listen for the rise & fall of a single breath. What I hear is stillness & silence in this dark parlor stuffed with loss. *Forgive me, Brother,* I whisper as I rise to leave. *I'm not ready today to say goodbye.*

Unread Memoir

The morning of her operation I told my sister in the hospital that I'd just finished a memoir of our chaotic childhood. I didn't want her to be alarmed when she read it and found that my memory of what happened differed from hers. "There's no single version of a shared past," I told her. "You know, Dad's a ghost to me now," she said. "Maybe your account of our childhood will bring back some of the good things I've forgotten."

For a long moment we held hands in silence. When the orderlies finally came and wheeled her down the empty corridor, she raised her hand to her lips, smiled and blew me a kiss. "I love you, too," I whispered in her direction. Then the stainless steel doors swung open and she disappeared from view, slipping quietly into the timeless Now, where none of our memoirs are unread, nothing is forgotten or unsaid.

Memorial

At the end of the service,
her brief life rendered to ashes,

portioned out to mourners
in containers of celadon,

a memento, they are told,
something tangible,

as if grief
could be held at

bay, death disarmed by
a gift of ashes.

Ice Storm

Early this morning
a bohemia of glass
outside the sunroom;

me, breathless,
a stranger
in my own country.

Winter Invocation

Dispersed by swirling winds
snow fell all night;
by morning, the limbs of trees outside
    the sunroom window sagged
under a thick layer of white.

Wedged like a frozen breath
between memory & absence,
I thought I glimpsed
    a gathering of ghosts—
was it a springing cedar bough, a wing,
a shiver of falling snow or just my
imagining? When I looked again
the ghosts had disappeared,
only the silence remained.

How long, Lord, before
you touch my winter mind with
Spring's long, warm, tendrils?

Apollo's Dream

Apollo,
confident in his craft,
master of his fears,
descends into the dank
cave where judges
cast their spells.

Sentenced
to an eternity
of probing eyes.

Hermes

Who is this arrogant stone deity
with the long beard,
surrounded by bronze lamps,
who demands we come
to his altar at evening,
fill our lamps with oil,
burn incense,
pay tribute in coin before
we are allowed to whisper
our questions in his ear,
with no guarantee of answers
unless we catch, by chance,
some vagrant rumor or voice
floating in air?

On Reading Miłosz

You wrote that even memory is under sentence
of death, described how the pitiless waters will

close over all of us, both living & dead, erase our
names & memories, every single, brilliant,

moment that made our lives vivid & unique,
washed away into a Lethian netherworld as

though it was all a cruel jest. Your grim
prediction made me shudder. Tell me it isn't so,

Czesław. Where did the music go?
Where did it come from?

I need to know, I need to know.

A WORLD APART

Fog

Driving to court
this morning,
the fog rose up,
plunging me into a night
streaked with moons
and comets,
all my bright intentions.

A Strange Feeling

As I slash
through stacks of divorce

files on my desk, lopping off
decades of life together,

children, homes, holidays,
good times, foul times,

with a flick of my pen,
I'm trespassing

on holy ground,
and when I see

lilies, turtle doves,
and golden rings on the

scrolled Certificates of Marriage,
the wedding day

comes shining back,
and sad eyes watch

as I scrawl my name
across their ghostly witness.

The Craftsman

On this blustery January morning the
judge longed to escape the courthouse,

enticed by the blizzard of white outside
his window & the inviting thought of taking

his children skiing, but he couldn't leave,
duty bound as he was cobbling together

awkward legal boxes for people's miseries,
the warped & knotty wood yielding only

grudgingly to the blunt tool of reason,
his distracted mind adrift in pure snow.

Déjà Vu

When the woman with four small children, delin-
quent husband, bill collectors pounding on the
door, bolted from the witness box out into the
chilling rain this morning, shouting, "It's not fair, I
can't take it any more," the judge smiled at his con-
stable's joke that "you'd have thought the court-
house was on fire," till he remembered how many
times he left the courtroom believing he had heard
alarm bells shrilling, and saw justice going up in
smoke.

The next day in court, a woman testified she'd paid
the fine on time, but the government office lost the
cheque and now her driving permit was suspended
and to get it back she'd have to pay a reinstatement
fee she couldn't afford. "Of course it's not fair," he
told her. "You should think about getting a lawyer,
and yes, I know it'll be costly, but in the circum-
stances it's all you can do."

How often did his pronouncements come to this:
little chipped and disfigured imitations of justice
gouged out of law?

Show Time

On the marquee today, a new drama.
Observe the lawyers
in their natural habitat—

that is to say,
on display. Regard
their furtive stalking style,
crouching behind words,
the dark intent beneath the smile.

Speared by the judge's piercing eyes.
Polite assassins. Under contract.

Courtroom Tableau

Two tired silver-haired rivals of
the court, wearing the knuckled

vocabularies of their trade, going
through the ritual of slugging it

out in the well of the courtroom
over an arcane point of law under

the impatient gaze of a judge
worried about his afternoon golf

date, everyone praying for a
quick knockout.

Tribal Customs

—for Justice Speyer

Lawyers love to beat dead horses;
when the horse won't move they

buy stronger whips, change riders.
Sometimes the government appoints

a committee to visit race tracks,
stables, paddocks, clubhouses—

all the favourite watering holes.
Invariably the committee will

set new standards for riding and
recommend that no one dismount,

which leads to the present
craze—a phenomenon that never

ceases to amaze—lawyers proud
in the saddle like Gary Cooper,

astride several dead horses harnessed
together for greater speed,

prancing on the same spot repeatedly
and going nowhere in a great hurry.

Sun Shower

I slouch out of the cold, hard mouth
of the courthouse where lawyers make
a feast of trouble, lost for the moment
in the ambivalence of judging others,
the pulley of the law still creaking in
my ears, half-nodding, half-forgetting
who I am,

to be startled awake by a cool breeze
whipping across my face, raindrops
flicking off my bare skin & high above,
wildly winging over the trees, a scraggle
of crows scrolling out my name.

Fugitive Light

Every day in court I hunch over my bench book
listening to the sputterings of lawyers & witnesses,

hastily scribbling down notes, trying to keep
up with the torrent of ploys & obfuscations,

hoping to discover the hidden lode of verity beneath
falsehoods & rehearsed stories, find a clear passage

through the cloudy words & bleak days; like
the frantic sparrow this morning who strayed into

the courtroom from a half-open window, circled
the room looking, like me, for an exit,

a glimmer of light on the wing.

Judicial Odyssey

Frothy rhetoric roils the air, arguments volley back
& forth with reckless abandon. We, the passengers,
huddle in the courtroom—a frail vessel that threatens
to capsize.

The voyage gathers its own darkness—days when I
hold my tongue, fear some of the passengers will
never reach safe harbor,

knowing too, that whatever thankless decision I make,
the conflict will not be permitted to rest; the appellate
court will weigh in and litigants will once again be
tossed into the gusting winds and punishing waves
of the law.

The Remains of the Day

Four-thirty of an afternoon,
    the day's disgruntlement over,
the judge closes his chamber
    door, shuts his eyes, tries
to blot out the rancorous words &
    drizzle of lies
he's left behind
    on the courtroom floor.

He doesn't want to speak
    or wring his mind anymore;
all he wants to do
    is sleep.

A Certain Image

haunted the judge's dreams.
Standing over a deep well
he grips the ankles of the guilty
and before he lets go
glimpses terror
on their faces.
Then, pity ticking in his ear,
he leans his head
into the rounded darkness,
waiting
for the splash.

Waiting in Silence

Thwarted & unhappy,
my hungry prayers
crumble like biscuits.

How I covet the holy
concentration of cows,
chomping in silence,
sturdy as ships.

The task of the day—
simple & profound,
learn how to pray.

My One Allotted Question

Lord,
by what whimsy of divine justice
did you allow
a man disposed to evasion
who sees but
dimly through the shadows
to sit on a glass throne
and judge others?

PARODIES OF HOLY WRIT

Toward a Definition of Law

Law dresses in black silks, wears a coat
of thick paint, curls her hair with a cork-
screw, never powders her face in public.

Law seldom writes in straight lines, loves
the fripperies of words, hums in riddles &
slant rhymes, commonly finishes a sentence

with "without prejudice" or "on the other
hand." The eyes of Law glow like radium,
her laughter, the sound of delirium.

Law rarely blushes, never says she's sorry,
shuns looking in the mirror, steers clear of
dark stairwells, long unlighted corridors.

Law

With its long-jawed vocabularies, archaic rituals &
sharp knives,

with its high-minded intentions & squabbling lawyers,
interminable delays & baffling gaps,

with rules that bend with the money, judgments
tainted with the sly odor of vengeance,

with the newly convicted begging for mercy &
wrongly convicted crying of innocence,

with divided heart & wrenching decisions,
I bequeath you this Blindfold of Justice.

The Swish of Silk

The cry of "Oyez, oyez,"
    the swish of silk & the
red-sashed judge's grand entrance,
    leery eyes lifting expectantly,
the judge's face
    a dark code
no one could decipher,
    the law an unreadable page
about to turn &
    time running out.

Jurors

slouch in the jury
box, stolid as rocks

under the bored
gaze of the judge,

rhetoric of counsel
breaking over them

in hissing waves,
the law grating on

their nerves; confused &
disoriented, they spin

in whirlpools of
indecision, praying

with the judge for a
quick verdict to

end the torture.

There Are Courtrooms

with dusky
   windows,

parodies of
   Holy Writ,

where plush
   arguments

rise like
   colored

balloons &
   blow away,

apathy, finer
   than talc,

sifts down the
   the long

afternoons in
   waning light,

dusts the
   immaculate

cuffs of counsel,
   the eye

of justice grey.

Dream Diorama

I.

Counsel hands me a brief of authorities, an inch thick. What I am given is not the summary of the law I requested, but an old recipe book of Boston sea food chowders. What to do? Counsel are waving their arms, clamouring for a decision. "This case has already dragged on too long," they chorus. I hesitate, but then I remind myself that sometimes a judge has to make do with what he has. I flip open the book, shocked to hear my voice begin: "This Cape Cod chowder has some unusual ingredients…"

II.

I'm just returning from the courthouse, trudging along the sidewalk in the rain, clutching the Law bundled in plain brown paper as though it were the last best hope for a sane world, when Basil Brick my neighbour, the loutish and zealous law reformer, leaps his white picket fence, the gleam of the fanatic in his eye. At the last moment I start to run, but it's too late. To my shock and amazement Brick springs into the air, clamps both hands on the bundle and wrests the Law free, makes a beeline for his home across the lawns. The last I remember before I'm jolted awake is his haughty voice: "Now I'll show them what the Law should be."

III.

After he let Winkie, the black Lab, out, the judge sat down at the breakfast table and opened the morning paper. CRIME IN FREEFALL. For months, such headlines had cast a long shadow over his colleagues on the bench. He phoned the police. "What's going on, Chief?" but the chief, nonplussed, suggested a spiritual revolution was afoot. With courtrooms deserted he and his colleagues polished old judgments, redecorated their chambers, concealed their foreboding under a facade of quips about "going on the dole." Everyone knew a crisis loomed: a torrent of letters and email harping on judges' salaries, accusing them of idleness. They began to consume quantities of coffee, experimenting with exotic beans and roasts. After a few weeks their usually erudite discourse was reduced to squabbles over Colombian Excelso versus Kenyan AA, Full City versus Italian roast, sounding more and more like jumpy addicts, wide awake, yet unbelievably tired.

IV.

After years on the bench, the old judge, a staunch believer in the law, reported to work, shocked to discover that nothing remained of the historic courthouse where he dutifully labored for years but a crumbling stone foundation. Stunned, he went over to a nearby park where a boisterous celebration was in progress—litigants, lawyers, even a few of his colleagues, milling around a huge bonfire, tossing law books and court files into the flames. "What's going on?" he shouted, an unusual touch of panic in his voice, but before anyone could respond he shuddered awake, looked at the clock beside his bed and remembered with a sigh of relief it was April Fool's Day.

How to Paint a Timorous Judge

Pose him behind a desk heaped with massive tomes. Garb him in grey, the official color of law. Catch the spirit of his vacillating voice as he pleads with litigants to settle. As his struggle to decide his cases was well known, try to capture his ambivalence by accenting the panic in his small, irresolute eyes when finally cornered to make a decision. With a last touch highlight the sheen on his brow and the wavering look on his face. His portrait, now ready for hanging, requires no identification. The nameplate can simply say: *The Judge*.

The River

After court the judges go down to the river.
They shed their sashes, their silk robes.
Stand on the shore naked.
Dip their pale swollen feet in the water.
The river moves quietly.
The judges breathe in great gulps of clean air.
The first thing they do is wash the blood from their hands.

LITTLE MERCIES

White Feather

During morning break
        his deputy came to him
in chambers
        holding a long
white feather.
        "I found it in the
courtroom," she said,
        astonished
as though evidence
        of a bird on the wing
had no place
        in the Halls of Justice.

One Question Too Many

After the lawyer asked the bespectacled witness in the blue suit about what he did for a living, silence fell over the courtroom. The lawyer repeated the question. "I'd rather not say," the witness answered.

That's when I stepped in to remind him that this was a court of law, that witnesses are obliged to answer all questions. "To tell the truth, Your Honour," he said, looking me in the eye, "I'm just putting the finishing touches on my plan to liquidate the national debt."

"The national debt?" I said. "How do you expect to do that?"

The witness smiled at me as though I were a child. "Now, Your Honour, I wouldn't be much of a businessman if I tipped my hand, would I?"

"I guess not," I replied. "Mum's the word."

Minnows

All eyewitnesses agreed
that the day of the accident
was warm and sunny.

The victim testified that
she entered the intersection
on a green light and the accused
struck the front of her car.

The accused testified that
he entered the intersection
on a green light and the victim
struck the front of his car.

The old lady rocking
on the veranda testified
that the accused definitely
ran the red light.

The young man on the Suzuki motorcycle
testified that the accused
definitely stopped
at the red light.

The pensioner strolling on the sidewalk
testified that everything happened so fast
he couldn't say what color the light was.

The judge remembered another sunny day
at Jackson's Creek and minnows
shimmering past
his small, awkward hands.

Impasse

Driving home after a hard day in criminal court
sentencing a motley line-up of repeat offenders,

the judge got stuck at a railway crossing—
a mile-long caravan of rolling stock: freight,

gondolas, hoppers, flatbeds, tankers, even
a three-tiered cattle wagon stacked with pigs,

snouts wedged between the grey slats
snuffling for air, eyes pierced with panic, the

caravan clicking along to the metallic heartbeat
of a bell hammering out the seconds, each car

bearing the same message: ANYROAD, ANYWHERE.

Random Graces

Even when weather turns cruel,
the light hard & brittle, everyone
locked in bleak winter thoughts,
shivering in their bones, unexpected
moments of grace appear—
children on the sidewalk,
heads tilted to gaze at eaves
of dripping ice needles, their
curious eyes startled by
the cold splash of wonder.

Buried in the Snow

—for Bob Zelinski

How odd I know
　　to overhear oneself say
at 3 o'clock
　　on a winter's day:
"We want the truth,
　　the whole truth &
nothing but the truth,"
　　a blizzard blowing
cold blue needles
　　outside the courtroom window.

A Momentary Distraction

In the middle of a long, tiresome case, the judge
glanced out the courtroom window at a train

in the distance rolling past with its caravan of empty
boxcars in tow, remembered the trains of his youth &

how he & his friends would hitch a free ride hopping
into the empty boxcars, struggle to maintain a solid

footing as the cars shook & swayed amidst the swirl
of cindery smoke, only to leap off at the last

moment—a balancing feat much easier, the judge
knew, than keeping the wobbly wheels of justice

on track in a legal arena where the rhetoric of war
abrades the nerves & lawyers pummel one another

behind a screen of glossy words, the law lurching
underfoot, a new direction at every swerve.

A New Disposition

When the judge with the curmudgeonly disposition opened court in the morning, lawyers shuddered, for he had a fearful reputation of never suffering fools gladly, tongue-lashing them mercilessly for the least gaffe or unpreparedness, his trenchant mind cutting through their spurious legal arguments like a two-edge sword, leaving them in total disarray, licking their wounds.

But after lunch and his customary two dry martinis his mind underwent a sea change, lost its beveled edges and he'd begin to sketch—his boyhood passion—filling page after page of his bench book with happy-go-lucky children's faces, glancing up from time to time at the lawyers, much to their bewilderment, with the sweet-tempered smile of an indulgent father.

Spring

After a long grey winter of
darkness and discontent,
clouds lift and
the judge, caught off guard,
allows his heart to step outside
    into grace:
a sweeping rush of green.

A Glassy Stillness

Even memory
is under sentence of death.
                    —Czesław Miłosz

Sky darkens imperceptibly,
rain stipples
the flat surface
of the pond,
drops falling
one by one
making tiny ripples,
each a memory
circling & widening,
water into water,
leaving only
a glassy stillness.

Early Morning at the Lake

I awake from
the tumult of nightly dreams,
my head in disarray.

On the horizon
a great blue heron
glides in silence across the bay.

Designated Dreamer

...and the dream outlasts
Death, and the dreamer will never die.
        —R.S. Thomas

I am your designated dreamer,
intimate like you with the history

of disappointment, steeped in the
shadowlands of sleep, one who

surfs the rag ends of dreams at
night to bring you news of your

buried self, wake you from your
dreamless bed, make you under-

stand there's nothing solid any-
where for you to stand on except

the dark rich earth
of your heart.

WHISPER OF DOUBT

Brief Epiphany

Driving to court along the Hanlon Expressway this spring morning, the sun peeks through the skeletal woods, skims the top of an embankment, winks off the cars speeding past, tinges the smoke from Sleeman's Brewery a pale orange. A few patches of dirty white snow still blur the edges of fields along the 401. A marsh hawk on a fence, poised & imperious, sounds off in the colorless air. By the time I reach the Milton ramp & glimpse the courthouse in the distance my spirits rise with the sun, now a radiant white coin, but I cannot alter or disguise the reality that I must enter the stormy badlands of the law where hair-trigger lawyers know how to put the lie to every false dream.

Monday Morning Blues

Entering the courthouse out of the bright
    epiphany of morning sunlight

you leaf through the file on your desk and, as is
    your custom, review

the salient facts of the young offender you're
    about to sentence.

Before the courtroom door groans open
    you steel yourself one last time

in front of the bathroom mirror, bury your
    qualms deep inside the thick

court file and stride into court hoping no one
    will hear your pulse racing

beneath your smooth silk robe, feel the blue
    torque of the law

clamping round your heart.

Caught in the Net

Only three days into this trial and already I'm in a sweat, for it's becoming apparent that the Plaintiff, a small fish in a big sea, will be swallowed up, bones and all, by the Leviathan Trust Company whom he dared to bite. As judge I cling to the raft of impartiality, hoping for a miracle—that the Plaintiff, like Jonah, will escape unscathed but, alas, it is not to be. My plea to settle is rejected and God, it appears, is in no mood for miracles. The case rolls on like a tidal wave as the net closes and I resign myself to my role as eviscerating shark of justice.

How I Spend My Time in the Law

—for James R. Elkins

I sit on a bench
    harder than stone

sniffing for clues, listening to
    witnesses, experts, lawyers

drone on,
    discovering the flaws

in their dry circumlocutions,
    the facts so cunningly

hidden from view,
    then finding

the crack in the wall
    of the law where

Justice peeks through
    I craft a judgment

that tries to sing true, one
    that I pray

I'll live not to rue.

A Bottomless List of Questions

After a wakeful night the judge arrived early at the ourthouse as was his custom. He brewed coffee, diverted his mind for a few minutes scanning the morning paper. He remembered that he'd forgotten to purchase tickets for the piano recital that evening, rang his wife; afterwards he glanced outside the window at the Niagara Ridge to catch the play of slanting sunlight on its jutting limestone cliffs. When he could no longer put it off, he reluctantly opened the file on his desk and the photo of the young female victim confronted him; that's when the horror of her grisly murder and his own suppressed anger came clawing back to rip away the mask of aloof dispassion he'd so carefully cultivated over the years, his armor against a bottomless list of questions, all beginning with *why*, questions he didn't know how to answer.

Whisper of Doubt

The judge saw his role not simply as an
arbiter of Right & Wrong methodically beat-

ing the drum of the law, rewards & punish-
ments rolling off his tongue, but also as a

footbridge between the legal system &
the hapless snared within its web, helping

accused & litigants cross over the muddy
ditches of their lives, showing them the

merciful face of Justice. Sometimes he'd
leave the courthouse, steps lighter than air,

feeling he'd made a difference, a small
contribution to the administration of

Justice. Only later in bed in the maw of
the night when stars cupped blue lips to

his ear, did he wonder if maybe there was
something he missed or didn't get right,

hear the whisper of doubt drawing near.

Nightmare

There are worse things than rendering good
judgments in language only lawyers love;

there are worse things than a judge's convoluted
syntax holding forth a parched interpretation of
the law pronounced in the holy name of Justice;

there are worst things than brooding over what
appellate judges might decide the law ought to be.

It's 3 a.m., after a restless night's pretense at sleep,
when all the judge's ill-considered judgments, each
of them wearing a long, resentful face, come trooping
into his bedroom to confront him, to speak a truth
he does not want to hear.

—inspired by Fleur Adcock

Undertow

After his appointment to the bench, the judge wanted to think his carefully constructed decisions would make the legal world a more human enterprise. But as the years sloshed and slipped along, disappointment began to set in. The tide of evil-doing continued to wash ashore, and the law made scant headway against the dark forces of decline and disintegration. Every day he saw vengeful litigants, their barbed hearts intact, trying to use the courts as a cudgel against their adversaries. Reasonable compromises he'd glued together to defuse family feuds often came unstuck. Everything he touched appeared provisional and expedient. On low days, he felt as if all his words were written in invisible ink.

One day leaving the courthouse he had a chilling thought: *The future awaits us all like a dark sun.*

Invisible Man

Day in, day out, he groans under the weight
of human folly, hammers out

tiny replicas of Justice on the anvil of the
Law, rewards and punishments

pouring from his mouth. Somewhere beneath
his judicial armour, he knows,

throbs a heart of flesh, but when he speaks,
only the Law moves his lips. Sometimes

he imagines himself a disembodied voice,
an artist on the high wire of right and wrong,

no net beneath him. His worse fear: take away
the silk robe & red sash, and he'll fall, no one
there to catch him.

Musings

After another case in court—
a brutal father, frustrated
by his daughter's inability to do
math, punished her with
a lit cigarette—I go home with
a sense of defeat.

At times like this I turn to
wishful thinking on the chance
it'll help me survive the misery
that encircles me.

I tell myself that being witness
to a flawed humanity I cannot
escape is not cause for despair.
No one appointed me the oracle
of Delphi.

Dog Day

Sirius, the dog star, arises with the sun
during the hottest time of the year.

In the judge's nightmare a mob
storms the courthouse, sacks
the great library, carts off
all the books to Hero Square where,
dancing around the raging pyre, it chants:
We want justice.

Driving to court that morning he observes
on the horizon a jet stream—a knotted
ball of yarn unravelling
like a tattered judgment—

                      wonders
what siren had lured him to this grief
of judging others.

The witness testified
that Robert, the fifteen-year-old
was a fine boy who never
did drugs or went to rock concerts,
the sort of boy
parents could be proud of,
always kind & cheerful.
Robert liked the elderly couple next door.

"The idea just popped into my head,"
he told the police.
The psychiatrist had no explanation.

After court he felt disoriented as though
stranded in some foreign train station
surrounded by unfamiliar luggage &
strange accents.

At home that evening he answered his wife's
greeting with a scowl, barely
spoke at dinner, flared
at the children for nothing.

Afterward, he lingered outside listening
to the cantillation of the frogs, tossed
a stone into the silver-black glass of the pond,
watched the surface quiver &
                    break to pieces,
waited for the reflection of moon & trees
                    to reassemble again,
rings to disappear &
              the pond return to stillness.

Dust of Indifference

Just as first snowflakes spiral
to their quiet death, unnoticed,

you fail to observe until too late
the tiny particles, finer than flour,

more toxic than asbestos, sifting
down through the querulous air

the long afternoons of courtroom
tedium, coating bench, bar, tables,

chairs, dockets, water jugs, laptops,
pens, with a thick layer of dust,

blinding the eyes of Justice
with a grey indifference.

A Judge's Life

is a history of lonely moments,
fingering slippery facts for clues,
decoding glyphs of law, perplexed &
vexed with doubt,
the weight of someone's future
tossing on his back and

after the case is closed and
judgment's jumped like a small capricious god
from the tip of his tongue and
punishment imposed,

going home in waning violet light
to lay awake in the sweaty palm of night,
some faceless someone's voice
still echoing in his mind,
a slow, drawing down of blinds,
the kind that never close.

A Judge's Yearning

Will I ever find
    that bright blue opening

in the murky sky of the law,
    learn to navigate

the choppy waters dividing
    being here

from being elsewhere,
    discover the winding

current back
    to the sea-clean air?

AN ICY NUMBING WIND

Baffling News

One noon as earth tipped toward spring, you quietly
departed on a journey into the darkness. You left no
clue, no explanation to appease the baffled mind, tak-
ing with you all the answers to the compulsory ques-
tion: *Why?*

After the police left and I had gone from shock to
numb, I ransacked the house—such is the mind's
hunger to understand—jewelry box, closets, dressers,
desk, books where you sometimes hid your thoughts,
every nook and hiding place, but found nothing, only
a house of *whys*.

With the news that you had flung wide the door to
oblivion, I faced a dark sea of dread, floundered at
night with fitful dreams, watching as I drowned under
waves of imagined guilt. A guilt that refuses to go
away.

Arctic Wind

That afternoon in Barbados two years before her sui-
cide, the judge and his wife sauntered hand in hand on
the beach, the blue flash of ocean all around them, lit-
tle suspecting how their world would forever change.
Back in their hotel room, she peered out the window
at a group of men in white jackets smoking and ban-
tering near the kitchen door. "They are government
spies," she whispered. Her face took on a pale faraway
look and for the rest of the vacation she stayed in bed,
pretended to listen to the rattle of the palm fronds, the
muffled thunder and hiss of the surf, rarely venturing
outside the bedroom.

At the airport as they queued to board the plane home
she turned to him and murmured: "There are secret
agents boarding the plane and they intend to arrest
you and take you to a concentration camp." Once they
were safely airborne the judge talked to her in the
most reasonable tone he could muster. "See, darling, I
wasn't arrested and there were no spies." Her sphinx
smile told him she wasn't convinced. Then she startled
him with her claim that she'd tossed her wedding ring
out the taxi window on the way to the airport because
she feared, as she put it, "the police would have used
that ring to torture you."

After they got home the judge noticed other disturb-
ing signs. The doctors diagnosis: Paranoid. Delusional

Depression. With rest and medication, they assured him, the symptoms would diminish over time. Such was the judge's need for a palatable fiction, this green feather of hope to cling to, he believed them.

When the blindsiding future came hurtling at him like an icy, numbing wind, no one could have been more shocked than he was.

The Journey On

Riven with loss over
    his wife's suicide
the old judge found
    himself alone
in a trackless,
    desolate field,
grief in his arms,
    distraught,
directionless,
    knowing dimly—
his only certitude—
    that he had no
choice but to
    befriend his pain,
and journey on,
    that the pain would
cleave to him
    to the end, rooted
as it was deep inside
    the rich dark earth
of his grieving heart.

Winter Longing

Now, when I
conjure up her memory,
a halo of cold
surrounds her face,
yet somehow she still
touches me—

like the snow that filled
my quiet wood
last evening with
the afterglow of her
presence and altered
the color of my mind,
made me reach out for her
pale white arms,
forget for the moment,
death's long, dark embrace.

The Architecture of Grief

Smaller and smaller archways leading
into a dark celestial dome, the
sucking sound of light
disappearing into
a million black
holes

Gutted Dreams

A few months after his wife's suicide, the judge accepted a guilty plea to arson from a man who'd torched the home he and his wife had built. The previous evening she'd told him the marriage was over, packed her suitcases and left with their two small children.

That evening, in the silence of his own wounded life, the judge studied the police photos of the caved roof, the charred walls, the scorched fieldstone fireplace, the litter of treasured keepsakes reduced to ashes, wondering how any of us survive the bonfires of this cruel world.

Black Frost

The witness testified that her husband of 25 years hanged himself from a beam in the basement of their home. "It's so unfair," she whispered. Rattled & nauseous, the judge called a recess as the reverberations from his wife's suicide came echoing back with such force he felt for a moment as though courthouse, lawyers, litigants, witnesses, books, water jugs, pens—the whole tangled apparatus of law—had been pitched into doubt, cast into an ever-widening gyre toward the black frost of receding stars, nothing for him to hold on to, but his own shattered heart.

Heart's Needle

Last evening
as darkness thickened
I walked down to the lake
to listen to the thrum
of raindrops, watch the ripples flatten,
fade into a break of moonlight
on the darkish sand. Slowly, slowly
I am learning to unclench my hand.

The Long Wait

This spring, for the first time in thirty
years, buds didn't appear on the paper

birch in the crevice of the rock by the shore.
Last summer it quaked like a young bride

in the breeze, swallows nested in the thick
dazzle of its green hair. Every April

it's worn the same hard appearance of death,
the empty spaces like the terrible longing

between people, but that never stopped its
soft fluent growth—the green-tipped nubbins,

then the pale yellow petals unfolding from
every twig. "The buds are always late,"

I say, touching a bare branch. My daughter
Ruth thinks I'm in denial. "Give up, Dad,

no one's coming back," she says. I kneel
on the rock, numbstruck, unwilling to disbelieve,

wondering how long I'll have to wait.

Black Cloud

The black cloud that hid
the face of the mountain
is drifting away;
if only seeing you again
could be that simple.

Limerick Lake Blues

Birds retreat to nests high
in the trees

on the silent staircase of air;
moon hides

its shining face from me; the
perishing fields of night

dwindle to blue specks in the
dark, an immensity

with no sides, no depth; nothing
grows in this waning light

except absence.

The Last Wish List

After the reading the young poet approached the judge with a question: "Why did you become a poet?" The judge, who had taken up poetry after his wife's death, had routinely answered that question before, but on this occasion his words crumbled in his mouth.

The young poet would have unaccounted years ahead to test the slopes of love, write her poems, compile her own list of squandered affections, taste the wormwood of failed dreams. When the judge was young he thought growing old a quaint illusion. Now his unfinished wish list began to unscroll in his head: keep evil at bay, disarm sharp tongues, dampen the rancour and volatile passions that infect the spirit, repair the world by applying the laws fairly and with compassion, learn the lost dialect of love, speak with the gentle voice of poetry and reconciliation—till he drew back, realized his mind had drifted into the deep, unchartable gulf between his own past and the young poet's future, that he hadn't answered her question.

The young poet, unfazed, had another question and still another.

THE JUDGE GROWS OLD

Sweet Longing

The old judge lifted the garlic jar to the light, jade-colored, ringed like Saturn, ash deposits on its fire face, a circlet of five air holes near the base. The potter's note said it was ripened in a river of fire—a two-chambered "Japanese style" climbing kiln—wood-stoked for twenty hours—a plain, but elegant artifact, glazed with love, destined to adorn someone's kitchen for years.

Leaving the studio, he felt strangely downcast thinking about all the time he'd spent peering down the fractious throats of Right & Wrong, looking for guilt or innocence, waking most days from a dream-tossed sleep, the first rays of pale sun poking through dusty glass, never knowing if he had created anything that would last.

The Past Still Lives

The old judge, his dream faltering, bears the mounting weight of his age. The law, some days, feels like a great millstone—the litigants spiteful, their lawyers quarrelsome. When he looks back across the mist of years he sees himself on a far, sunlit hill, a young man, climbing.

A Judge's Prayer

Too long I've been
a bedfellow with trouble,
immersed in the crabbed
world of law,
cast down day after day
by the greed & guile
of the human tribe,
often losing my bearings,
bruised & bitter,
a desperate prayer
on my lips.

Hasty Note from a Dizzy Planet

Internet, Facebook, iPad, texting, smartphone, everyone's nerves raked by a tsunami of words, silenced by the blare of what is not being said. Let those who have faith in how we now live step forward.

I, for one, have begun to unravel, don't know how much more of this I can take. Sometimes I think of digging a hole and climbing in. Recently I told my wife, who has witnessed all my aberrant eruptions, that if the pain becomes unbearable I might throw myself into a lake of molten lead.

"You know, don't you, what this means?" she said. "You're getting old."

Lull of Night

After another day of discord riddled
with treacherous language, the old

judge, sheet lightning flashing outside
his window, listens through the night

to rain rattling against glass, ponders
the abstract follies of the law & its chronic

inability to chart the ways of the human
heart, tries for brief moments to hold

on to the stony stillness that would keep
him anchored before a new day arrives &

he lumbers back through the portals of
the courthouse, carrying another heavy

sack of broken promises.

Fissures of the Mind

The old judge, who was known for his caring,
compassionate nature, was presiding over

a hard-fought criminal case when he observed
a carpenter ant crawling across his bench. The

ant paused, kicked its forelegs and looked
back at him as though asking why he wasn't

paying attention to the case, making him
feel guilty. As the judge leaned over, blew

the ant off its spindly legs onto the courtroom
floor, then crushed it underfoot, the lawyers

watched in silence, mouths agape. When the
judge glanced up to find them staring

at him he smiled sheepishly and said, "Call it
a small fissure of the mind."

The old judge in sentencing hard-core criminals
had grown into the practice of not looking them

in the face. He realized he was in the grip of an
ancient taboo: never look evil directly in the eye.

What the old judge was slow to realize is that
he had his own cache of molten darkness. Sometimes

looking in the mirror he'd glimpse a broken face
he had trouble recognizing as his own.

&

As the judge grew old he became less &
less patient with the verbal tumult of court—

an echo chamber of jangled nerves and prickly
words careening back & forth. At the end

of the day he'd go home, a headache creeping
up on him, to seek refuge in his garden,

doze under the large catalpa tree in slanted
evening light lulled into the fold between day

and night, dreaming he could hear holy voices
from the other side of silence, his mind

calmed, his headache soothed.

❦

When he finished his last case the judge
promised a speedy decision, but

as days slipped by he kept postponing
the day of judgment. After a month

the facts began to shift & turn,
grinding against each other

like tectonic plates, changing shape.
After several more months the legal

issues blurred and melded. His bench
book was little help; notes jotted down

in the heat of courtroom battle had
become indecipherable, colder than a dead

toad. That's when the judge realized he'd
drifted far beyond the edge of memory,

was hopelessly locked in a dark box with
scarcely a blade of light, the bright

house of reason he'd so long inhabited
slowly closing its doors to him forever.

Cargo of Dreams

The judge was too old & wise to
believe everyone would follow

the little legal verities that wobbled
off his tongue; sometimes fleeing

the courthouse sunk so low by
the drip-feed of constant lies he'd

listened to all day—not even a
reasonable facsimile of "the truth,

the whole truth & nothing but the
truth"—he'd rush home to climb into

bed, wait impatiently for sleep to
drift up like a little boat with its

cargo of dreams to bear him away,
knowing through it all that the respite

would be fleeting; come daylight &
the return of the unadorned truth of

living, his old scuffed shoes would
still be there to bring him back to earth.

Instructions to the
Photographer of a Retiring Judge

Bring the lens up close;
a straight frontal view is fine;
be kind, or if you must, candid.

Forgo unusual lighting, the clever
euphemisms of the dark room.
Capture his studied pose,
let him not appear so stiff, but
quietly disengaged
with a touch of gravitas.

Show the accoutrements of office—
black silk robe, red sash, starched winged collar—
the panoply of power he secretly loved.

Catch, if possible—the skeptical look,
the thin firm mouth, the ice-blue eyes—
the illusion of a person hidden behind the mask.

Highlight his crown of luxuriant, silvery hair,
the ragged seams of what passed for living on his face.

Do justice to him if you can. If not,
let morning light tell all.

Memories

haunted the old judge, rolled around
his head like polished pebbles: the look

of her hippie leather sunhat as she
stooped to pick daisies on a sunlit hill,

her limbs a clear calligraphy against
a milk-blue sky, the tears that ran

down her cheeks that morning in the
open field when she told him all was

forgiven, that she was ready to try
again. No inkling then with death so

far away, of all the might-have-beens,
the small, cold betrayals that lay ahead

between first light and the slow return
of evening—the long & slippery

footbridge of love.

Last Judgment

Three days before his swearing-out the judge dreamed he was arrested and hauled before the court. "You have been found guilty of public mischief," the old cantankerous Chief Judge, a former colleague, ruled, "for writing dull and consistently bad judgments for many years and exposing both the Bench and the Law to ridicule and contempt. In accordance with statutory law governing judges I hereby sentence you to be incarcerated, stripped and strapped to the floor naked. Thereupon all your witless and addled-brained judgments (which not to limit the foregoing shall include rulings, interlocutory orders, non sequiturs, solecisms, slips of the tongue, politically incorrect pronouncements, together with your large collection of irrelevant *obiter dicta*) shall be stacked on your supine body one tiny miscarriage of justice after another till the dead weight of your accumulated blunders shall turn you into a thin replica of your former portly, blustery self, speechless and incapable of ever lifting a pen again. Only then will you be released back to the deserved obscurity of private life. Do you have anything to say?"

A Sad Tale

The old judge woke one morning,
his heart had flown, sprung from its rib cage
without a trace
in the dead of night while he
lay dreaming
of the wheel of perfect justice.

A note on the bedroom door:
After years of neglect,
I can't take it any more.

The Mystical Foundation of Authority

The reverse side also has a reverse side.
—Japanese proverb

For years the judge loved the interplay
of language & logic, saw them as tools
to probe the real world, discover "the truth
the whole truth & nothing but the truth,"

until, that is, he studied linguistics and
learned from Wittgenstein that reality's
a figment of the mind, true & false,
social artifacts & all law—a matter of politics.

Now, on wet autumn evenings he drifts
about his house looking for dustballs, leans
against the gloomy furniture, ponders the dialects
of rain, the bat-squeaks in the walls,

the strange collusion of it all.

Power of the Breeze

In the beginning the judge had trouble
making up his mind, reserved most judgments.
Then he grew convinced most lawsuits were
frivolous, spiteful & driven by greed—a waste
of his time and the taxpayer's dollar.
"This case shouldn't be before the court."
He'd get migraines & stomp out of court
in the middle of a case.

Nowadays on most afternoons the judge
can be found on the grassy hummock behind his
house, indulging his boyhood passion: flying kites.
"Isn't it amazing," he will tell you, gazing
at their long tails twisting in the blue,
"what a little breeze can do?"

Checkmate

For years the judge
scrawled his signature across
page after page of grief & guile. Now,
cold and shuddery, he wonders
if the apple
on his bedroom window sill,
yellow & wrinkled,
still dreams of orchards,
a lost sun.

The Night Moth Returns

Between stars and screen
the moth,
with iridescent body
and seven white notches
on delta wings,
      listens
to the cantillations
of the frogs,
a prisoner like me,
caught in the shadows.

GOING HOME

Autumn Doldrums

The wind that blows is all anybody knows.
      —Henry David Thoreau

Certain names cut deep:

Teetaw with chalk white skin begging
us to be with her at the end, help her
concentrate on dying;

my friend Morley, an oracle of fair weather
all his life, cursing the storms that darkened
his path;

and brilliant and kind Emma, a teacher and
friend who dropped the word "better" from
her lexicon of hope, severed the knot that
bound her to her pain.

Letter by letter the wind gouges their
memory across my heart.

Desertion

Mother   father   wife   sisters
relatives   friends   neighbors—
pulled mercilessly, even randomly
from the ranks of the living,
conscripted into that
    last dark voyage.

Baffled, I am left to endure
a world I scarcely recognize—
forced to live this remorseless
    unravelling of the heart.

Sunset

Another evening drawing in
across the lake as we gather
by the window to see the spent
sun burning deep inside the
trees, cottage wall aflame.
Compassed by doubt & dark I
try to cup the dancing fire.
"Shame it doesn't stay," I say,
forgetting in my heart's desire
that someone, somewhere on this
turning globe is always catching
gold, the dazzling coin spinning
from eye to eye, the air beyond
our darkening hands holier than rain.

A Quiet Haven

Not anymore the steep edge
of the field, the wet sedge,

not anymore the pins of light in
polar night;

I have fitted my hand to the latch,
the sloping roof, found

that haven in the mind where
kisses, bread, talk

are cradled, the gravity of the
world lifted,

a place to hold onto against
the long hours of emptiness,

the irremediable cold.

Flawed Master

Keeper of the holy order of things;
master of jurisprudence;
explainer of the changing rules that keep us
safe & fit for human habitation save
the ones that never change & confound us most,
rules that tell us what to live for.

Turning 80

Showers abbreviate the air
on this third ring of the sun;
a cloud-capped arch morphs
into a rainbow.

As the speed of life confounds me, I teach
my grey heart to sing: *go slow, go slow, go slow,*
and learn to inhale, exhale
in the blazing Now of this, our once-only,
gratitude—a blessing white as vapour
on my breath.

Each day, the last day.

Dark Wood

In the middle of a life is a dark wood.
                    —Dante

Celestial navigation awry,
we slog along, waist-deep in
darkness, no wayside inns,
no alibis, our blood turned
cold as ice water.

There's nothing we can do but
name the path we took, plead
our case, beg the mercy of
the court.

Insatiable Quest

This morning a muffled drumbeat against the
    bedroom window wakened me.

Outside, a robin, feathers askew & wobbly,
    teetered on a branch trying

to catch his balance. The windowpane reflected
    back his orange vest, wet

green stalks of trees & milk-blue sky. That
    morning & the next & next

the bird thumped against the glass, each time
    knocked back by the

same invisible wall, ruffled & shaken, till at last
    it dawned on me that it would

never give up; like us, caged in skin, who long
    to beat our way heavenward,

he'd keep trying to break free, enter that dim
    lush paradise, prepared,

if need be, to go on forever.

Deliverance

Haunted by
    old regrets,
I traverse the burnt
    ground of memory,
praying for
    an end to darkness.

Fully awake now,
    light creeps back,
leaves catch the sun,
    owls return
to nest.

Prayers answered,
the white night recedes.

Finding Words

Out of the dying embers,
fire-fly sparks   skitter
into the night;

baffled by stirrings
deep within me
of infinite tenderness
for our flickering little light,
I wonder how I'll ever fire into language
the tall starry strangeness
of it all.

Wintry Radiance

Snow leavens a grey sky, lays
heavy on the gnarly black branches
of the old apple tree in my backyard.

Morning light slowly erases
the night's dark memories, but
having stayed long on this earth,
I am fixed with the knowledge
I must now live with the ghosts
swarming back to haunt me.

I step out into the new day, wait
for snow to softly touch my bare
hands, let it blanket me
with white forgetfulness.

Poet's Haven

Who would have thought my shriveled heart
Could have recovered greenness?
                    —George Herbert

And now in winter,
   after such dire depletion,
with so many fires
   banked,
this dry wood
   rekindles
my green words,
   sleep's little darkness
folding into
   amazing light.

Listen, Friend

I write these poems
    for you who whisper
why.

Am I nothing but
    a stuffed seabird,
tweeting to myself,
    my wingless words
greyer than pebbles
    on a deserted shore?

Take the poems, I say,
    toss them skyward, watch
them catch the sun,
    relight once more
that fire on your tongue.

The Art of Canoeing

—for John Hicks

requires quiet hands,
hands that hear
the music
of the paddle,

hold the wood
of the world gently.

Going Home

Be patient.
We are going home.
It is not far. We are rocking
in the great belly of the ship.
No light cracks the dark sea, but
the ship is strong, the voyage
will not be long.

We will arrive early.
It will be morning. We will
rub our unshelled eyes, see
the shore rise.
We will untangle our bones & play
in the lemon groves, dwell
in a white house near blue water.
There will be time. Be patient.
We are going home.

EPILOGUE

Swervings of the Heart

When my wife Mary and I got married in 1961, the future looked uncertain. Our decision to move to a small town in Ontario entailed her giving up a promising career as a fashion illustrator in Toronto. Our finances were precarious. And it wasn't long before we had a family to support.

Eventually things improved. My law career prospered and we bought our first home. Our children turned out to be happy, healthy, and bright. We enjoyed many of the "good things" in life. In 1983, I accepted an appointment to the bench. A few months later, family and friends gathered at the local church to help us celebrate the renewal of our marriage vows. We considered ourselves fortunate.

On April 8, 1990, a sunny Palm Sunday afternoon, everything changed. That was the day the police came to our door and told us my wife of twenty-eight years had jumped to her death at Niagara Falls.

Several witnesses observed her climb the parapet of the observation platform, camera in hand, drop her shoulder purse to the ground and holding her nose—she always pinched her nose before plunging into water—leap into the Niagara River, floating on her back, eyes open, blank expression on her face, no struggle or cries as the strong current swept her over the rim of the Falls eleven stories down into the icy gorge below. Her body has never been found.

The foundation of my existence collapsed. Even to this day several decades later, my children and I still feel the aftershock. Why, I asked. What could I have done differently?

For a long time after her suicide I wrestled with the question: What does God mean when a good person takes their life? I grew acutely aware of the feeling of God's absence and the unfairness that runs through all of life like a fault line. Inside I was tender and raw. Not long after Mary's death a young woman appeared in my court. She testified that her husband hanged himself from a beam in the basement of their home. Instantly her words unleashed a flash flood of emotion that drove me from the courtroom, tears in my eyes.

Remorse and confusion led me to seek answers. I immersed myself in the work of C.G. Jung, began to track my dreams. I started a journal and tried to come to grips with what had happened.

Then, in the summer of 1995, visiting an aunt in the Laurentians, I wrote my first poem. And then another and another. It was as if a dam burst, releasing years of pent-up feelings, painful childhood memories, unhealed adolescent wounds, intermingled with the debris of bereavement. I wrote about my frustrations on the Bench—the human face of law. Before long I'd accumulated a sizable collection of poems.

My poems would have gathered dust in a drawer but for my daughter Mira, who one morning mentioned a poetry workshop by Susan Musgrave, the well-known Canadian poet, to be held at the Lake of Bays in the summer of 1996. Encouraged by my children, I decided to go.

Susan Musgrave generously agreed to read my manuscript of poems. Imagine my surprise the next morning when I heard her say, "We've got to find you a publisher." She even offered to write an introduction. Barry Callaghan, the distinguished publisher and poet, to whom Susan had referred me, was equally enthusiastic. My first book of poetry, *Silver Mercies*, was published by Exile Editions in 1997. Mary's suicide broke the frozen seas within me, and collection after collection of poetry followed. Poetry rekindled my commitment to my work as a judge.

One pleasant surprise was the positive reaction of my colleagues on the bench. While judges and poets both work with words, for lawyers and judges words are primarily utilitarian, tools to build arguments and render judgments. For poets, words are windows for "intense seeing," as the poet Lorna Crozier put it.

I had worked almost exclusively with the left side of the brain, the seat of logic and common sense. Bounded by technical legal reasoning, knowledge of the law, and the restraints of precedent, I made little room for literary imagination, intuition, and emotion. While judges struggle to preserve the "human touch," the reality is they are in the unenviable business of judging others. In my poetry, I came to see that we are all on a common journey toward death, and that all human judgments are at best one-sided and incomplete.

My wife's suicide gave me a chance to see life from a different perspective—as one who is judged, one who bears the weight of guilt and shame. I learned that to forgive oneself is the precondition of compassion for others. By learning to "see behind the shutters normally drawn over the human face," as Al Purdy wrote, poetry helped me to connect with others, even in the bleak and impersonal Siberia of the courtroom.

As a judge, I redoubled my efforts to balance mercy and justice—always a delicate task. Chinks in the legal system I represented now stood out more starkly. To avoid cynicism, the occupational hazard of judging, I constantly had to remind myself that people are more different than they sometimes appear in the distorted mirror of the courtroom.

The plight of others began to touch me deeply. I recall the case of a major bank that sought judgment on a debt against a woman with three small children whose husband had abandoned them after squandering the funds on drugs and gambling. The woman who co-signed the promissory note lived in a dingy apartment, and was struggling to eke out an existence for herself and the children on \$25,000 a year as a clerk in a department store, with no support and no savings. Though counsel for the bank presented a strong case I dismissed the lawsuit, citing "duress and coercion" in the co-signing of the note. Almost immediately counsel sprang to his feet. "But, Your Honour," he began, but I cut him off. "You can't squeeze blood from a stone," I barked. "If you don't like my decision, appeal." Alone in chambers afterwards, I began to wonder if I hadn't been playing God with my stern-voiced pronouncements.

I began to seek ways to encourage litigants to settle. One morning a married couple appeared in court, each brandishing a long list of complaints against the other. Though seated only a short distance apart, their stiff posture and averted eyes gave no hint that they even acknowledged the other's presence. Detecting a residue of tenderness in their voices when they spoke of each other, I seized the opportunity to suggest they talk privately in a witness room to see if they could iron out their differences. At 11 a.m. my court constable said, "I think they're talking." A half-hour later she returned. "Guess what, I heard them laughing." At the noon break the constable entered my chambers, a broad smile on her face. "You won't believe this, Your Honour, but they're going out to lunch together." And when court reconvened at 2 p.m., the lawyers rose to announce that the parties had amicably settled all their issues. That day I left the courthouse knowing I'd made a small contribution to the administration of justice.

One of the most gratifying moments of my years on the bench was a letter I got from a young man I'd sentenced to reformatory. He wrote me how his life had completely turned around, that he planned to get married, and it was something I'd said to him in court that had made the difference. For days my feet barely touched the ground. What had I done? Nothing extraordinary except step out of my role as judge for a moment and talk to him as a fellow human being.

Poetry gave me the courage to speak my deepest yearnings and to venture forth toward those invisible angels who feed our hunger for justice. Ancient Chinese wisdom says it best—poetry is like being alive twice. Poetry gave me a second chance. In a sense, poetry saved my life.

ACKNOWLEDGMENTS

A version of this book, entitled *The Juried Heart,* was published in the United States by Pleasure Boat Studio in 2015.

The poems in *The Juried Heart* and *Oblique Verdicts* were selected from *The Kid from Simcoe Street: A Memoir and Poems* (Exile Editions, 2012), the *Legal Studies Forum* in collections titled *Designated Dreamer, All the Broken Places,* and *The Juried Heart,* and from the following collections published by Exile Editions: *Silver Mercies* (1997), *The Raggedy Parade* (1998), *The Ancient Pedigrees of Plums* (1999), *The Way Everyone Is Inside* (2000); *Flying Home Through the Dark* (2001), *How to Bribe a Judge: Poems from the Bench* (2002), *Forced Passage: A Short History of Hanging* (2005) and *Dreamworks: New and Selected Poems* (2008).

"Swervings of the Heart" was first published in John B. Lee (ed.), *Tough Times: When the Money Doesn't Love Us* (Windsor, Ontario: Black Moss Press, 2010).

ABOUT THE AUTHOR

James Clarke was born in Peterborough, Ontario, attended McGill University and Osgoode Hall. He practiced law in Cobourg, Ontario before his appointment to the Bench in 1983 where he served as a judge of the Superior Court of Ontario. He is now retired and resides with his second wife, Kathy, in Guelph, Ontario.

Clarke is the author of eight collections of poetry published by Exile Editions, and three memoirs: *The Kid from Simcoe Street* (Exile Editions, 2012), *A Mourner's Kaddish: Suicide and the Rediscovery of Hope* (Novalis, 2006), *L'Arche Journal: A Family's Experience in Jean Vanier's Community* (Griffin House, 1973). In addition, the *Legal Studies Forum* of the University of West Virginia law school has published nine collections of James Clarke's poetry.